Contents

Introduction

As the weather warms up, the temptation grows to not only eat outdoors, but to cook there, too. And, for creating relaxed meals, the barbecue proves itself the perfect partner. *Make Me Barbecue* is packed with more than 55 easy, flavoursome recipes that will inspire you to move your kitchen outdoors.

Barbecuing has to be one of the most straightforward and enjoyable ways to cook and the techniques needed to get the best out of it are simple and quickly learned. Within a relatively short cooking time, a subtle smokiness will have permeated your food, adding another dimension to your culinary repertoire. Juicy beef burgers, lemon- and oregano-infused octopus and succulent pork ribs and whole fish are all within your grasp when cooked on the barbecue—and the ease of cleanup is just another bonus.

Don't limit your use of the barbecue to summery days because it isn't just a warm-weather appliance. A beautifully cooked pork loin with a fig and pecan stuffing and crunchy crackling is easy to achieve on the barbecue and ticks all the boxes for a cheering winter's dinner.

The basics chapter at the back of this book contains extra flavour-enhancing spice rubs, marinades and sauces to accompany your chosen hero ingredients. Use them as inspiration to create your own favourites and expand on the recipes featured.

So, turn off your oven, put away the pots and pans, get out your tongs and take a step outside.

Beef & veal

Marinated beef ribs in dark ale & mustard

Preparation time: 10 minutes (+ 2 hours marinating time)
Cooking time: 50 minutes
Serves: 4

4 beef spare ribs (about 2 kg/4 lb 8 oz in total),
  halved (see tip)
125 ml (4 fl oz/½ cup) dark ale beer
2 tablespoons brown sugar
60 ml (2 fl oz/¼ cup) cider vinegar
2 fresh small red chillies, seeded, finely chopped
2 tablespoons ground cumin
1 tablespoon wholegrain mustard
20 g (¾ oz/1 tablespoon) unsalted butter
roasted potatoes and steamed asparagus, to serve

1 Arrange the spare ribs in a shallow non-reactive dish. Put the beer, sugar, vinegar, chilli, cumin and mustard in a medium bowl, stir well to dissolve the sugar and pour over the ribs. Turn to coat, then cover and marinate in the fridge for at least 2 hours or overnight.

2 Preheat half a covered barbecue to medium (see tip). Put the ribs and marinade in a large, shallow roasting tin and place on the barbecue over the burners that aren't turned on. Lower the lid and cook for 50 minutes for medium or until cooked to your liking (you should have about 125 ml/4 fl oz/½ cup of liquid left in the roasting tin). Transfer the ribs to a plate.

3 While the barbecue is still hot, put the roasting tin with its juices over direct heat to warm through. Use a whisk to beat in the butter then season with salt and freshly ground black pepper. Arrange the ribs on plates and drizzle with the warm sauce. Serve with the roasted potatoes and steamed asparagus with any remaining sauce passed separately.

TIPS: Ask your butcher to cut each rib in half as it is very difficult to do this at home.

You will need a covered barbecue for this recipe.

To cook on your barbecue using indirect heat, preheat one half of the barbecue with the burners at opposite ends. Cook food in the middle of the barbecue where the burners aren't operating. For a small barbecue, preheat half the barbecue on one side and place the food on the other side where the burners are turned off.

Italian beef burger

Preparation time: 15 minutes (+ 20 minutes chilling time)
Cooking time: 10 minutes
Serves: 4

500 g (1 lb 2 oz) minced (ground) beef
20 g (¾ oz/⅓ cup, lightly packed) fresh breadcrumbs
1 egg
2 tablespoons finely chopped basil
2 tablespoons black olive tapenade
1 tablespoon vegetable oil, plus extra, for brushing
1 large red onion, thinly sliced into rings
4 x 100 g (3½ oz) ciabatta rolls, split, toasted
40 g (1½ oz) baby rocket (arugula)
2 large roma (plum) tomatoes, thickly sliced

Garlic aioli
85 g (3 oz/⅓ cup) whole-egg mayonnaise
1 garlic clove, crushed
2 teaspoons freshly squeezed lemon juice

> **TIP:** Shape the beef patties according to the size of your bread rolls. The cooking time will vary depending on the thickness of the patties.

1 Combine the minced beef, breadcrumbs, egg, basil and half the tapenade in a large bowl and mix until well combined. Season with salt and freshly ground black pepper. Shape the mixture into four patties (about 10 cm/4 in wide and 2 cm/¾ in thick) (see tip). Refrigerate for 20 minutes or until firm.

2 Meanwhile, to make the garlic aioli, put all the ingredients in a small bowl and mix until well combined. Season with freshly ground black pepper. Cover and refrigerate.

3 Lightly brush barbecue flat plate with a little extra vegetable oil and preheat to medium–high. Cook the patties for 3–4 minutes each side or until browned and just cooked through. Meanwhile, place the onion on the barbecue flat plate with the patties and drizzle with the vegetable oil. Cook the onions, tossing occasionally, for 4–5 minutes or until golden.

4 Place the toasted roll bases on plates. Spread with half the aioli. Top with half the rocket, the patties, tomato and grilled onion. Top with a dollop of the remaining aioli and tapenade and the remaining rocket. Top with the toasted roll lids and serve.

Barbecued sirloin steak in bagna cauda marinade

Preparation time: 10 minutes
Cooking time: 5 minutes
Serves: 4

3 thick beef sirloin steaks (about 900 g/2 lb
   in total) (see tip)
125 ml (4 fl oz/½ cup) extra virgin olive oil
2 drained anchovy fillets, finely chopped
2 garlic cloves, crushed
4 thyme sprigs
finely grated zest and freshly squeezed juice
   of ½ lemon
350 g (12 oz/2 bunches) asparagus, trimmed
4 ripe tomatoes, sliced, to serve
crusty bread, to serve

1 Preheat barbecue flat plate to high. Brush the steaks
with 2 teaspoons of the olive oil.
2 Heat 2 tablespoons of the remaining olive oil in a small
roasting tin on the barbecue. Add the anchovies and cook for
3 minutes or until the anchovies melt. Add the remaining olive
oil, the garlic and thyme to the tin and allow to stand on the
barbecue until warm. Remove from the heat and stir in the
lemon zest and juice.
3 Season the steaks with salt and freshly ground black pepper
and cook, turning only once, for 1–2 minutes each side for rare,
or until cooked to your liking. Place the steaks in the roasting
tin and loosely cover with foil. Allow to stand for 2 minutes.
Turn the steaks and stand, covered, for another 2 minutes
or until rested and infused with the oil.
4 Meanwhile, cook the asparagus on the flat plate for
4–5 minutes or until lightly charred and tender. Halve
diagonally.
5 Thickly slice the steaks. Arrange the tomato, asparagus
and steak on plates and drizzle with the warm marinade.
Serve immediately with the crusty bread.

TIPS: You could ask your
butcher to cut a thick
sirloin steak and cook it
in one piece. It will take
longer to cook and to rest.

Bagna cauda is a
traditional Italian method
of adding flavour to cooked
vegetables. Here, the
method is applied to meat.
Instead of marinating
the meat before you cook
it, you do it afterwards
while it's resting.

Barbecued T-bone steak with roasted garlic butter

Preparation time: 10 minutes (+ standing time)
Cooking time: 25 minutes
Serves: 4

4 beef T-bone steaks (about 550 g/
  1 lb 4 oz each)
2 teaspoons olive oil
barbecued potatoes and green salad,
  to serve

Garlic butter
2 tablespoons rock salt
1 whole garlic bulb
2 teaspoons olive oil
150 g (5½ oz) butter, softened
2 tablespoons roughly chopped flat-leaf
  (Italian) parsley
freshly ground white pepper

TIP: Bringing the steaks to room temperature is an important step. The steak will cook more evenly, resulting in the centre being cooked to your liking without overcooking the outside. The cooking time will depend on the thickness of the steaks.

1 Remove the steaks from the fridge and bring to room temperature (see tip).

2 To make the garlic butter, preheat barbecue grill to medium–high. Place the rock salt on a 20 cm (8 in) square double sheet of foil. Break up the garlic into single cloves and place on the rock salt, drizzle with the olive oil and seal tightly. Place on the grill and cook for 10–15 minutes or until the garlic is soft. Remove the foil parcel and set aside to cool slightly. Increase the barbecue to high. Once the garlic is cool enough to handle, squeeze the flesh from the garlic cloves and combine with the butter and parsley. Season with salt and the white pepper. Set aside.

3 Make sure the grill is very hot. Season the steaks generously with sea salt and drizzle with the olive oil. Cook for 2–3 minutes each side for medium-rare or until cooked to your liking (see tip). Transfer the steaks to a clean plate, loosely cover with foil and set aside in a warm place to rest for 5 minutes.

4 Serve the steaks with the garlic butter spooned on top along with the potatoes and salad.

Tomato pesto beef skewers

Preparation time: 20 minutes (+ 30 minutes soaking time)
Cooking time: 10 minutes
Serves: 4

> 60 g (2¼ oz/¼ cup) bought tomato pesto
> 1 tablespoon freshly squeezed lemon juice
> 750 g (1 lb 10 oz) beef rump steak, cut into
>   2 cm (¾ in) pieces
> 3 small zucchini (courgettes), cut into 1 cm
>   (½ in) thick rounds
> 2 small red capsicums (peppers), seeded,
>   cut into 2 cm (¾ in) pieces
> lemon wedges, to serve

1 Soak eight wooden skewers in cold water for 30 minutes to prevent scorching.

2 Combine the pesto and lemon juice in a medium bowl. Add the steak and toss to coat. Thread the steak and vegetables alternately onto the skewers. Season with salt and freshly ground black pepper.

3 Preheat barbecue grill to medium–high. Cook the skewers, turning occasionally, for 8–10 minutes or until the vegetables are just tender and the beef is medium or until cooked to your liking. Serve the skewers with the lemon wedges.

Cajun beef ribs

Preparation time: 10 minutes (+ 20 minutes standing time)
Cooking time: 50 minutes
Serves: 4

    1 tablespoon dried onion flakes
    2 teaspoons smoked paprika
    1 teaspoon chilli powder
    2 teaspoons dried oregano
    2 teaspoons finely chopped thyme leaves
    1 teaspoon finely grated lime zest
    2 garlic cloves, crushed
    60 ml (2 fl oz/¼ cup) olive oil
    1.5 kg (3 lb 5 oz) beef spare ribs
    barbecued corn, and lime wedges, to serve

1 Put the onion flakes, spices, herbs, lime zest, garlic and olive oil in a small bowl and mix until well combined. Put the spare ribs on a large tray and brush all over with the spice mixture.
2 Preheat barbecue grill to high. Cook the ribs, turning, for 8 minutes or until browned all over. Turn the burners under the ribs off and leave the remaining burners on low. Cook the ribs, covered with the barbecue hood, using indirect heat, for 40 minutes for medium or until cooked to your liking. Transfer the ribs to a clean plate, loosely cover with foil and set aside in a warm place for 20 minutes to rest.
3 Use a sharp knife to cut the rib slabs into single ribs. Serve with the corn and lime wedges.

Mustard veal cutlets

Preparation time: 10 minutes (+ 2 hours marinating time and standing time)
Cooking time: 10 minutes
Serves: 4

60 g (2¼ oz/¼ cup) wholegrain mustard
60 g (2¼ oz/¼ cup) dijon mustard
4 garlic cloves, crushed
2 tablespoons olive oil
60 ml (2 fl oz/¼ cup) beef or chicken stock
1 tablespoon oregano leaves
2 teaspoons thyme leaves
4 veal cutlets (about 250 g/9 oz each)
vegetable oil, for brushing
potato salad, to serve

1 Combine the mustards, garlic, olive oil, stock and herbs in a bowl. Brush ¼ of the mustard marinade over both sides of the cutlets, reserving the remaining marinade. Put the cutlets on a plate, cover with plastic wrap and place in the fridge to marinate in the fridge for 2 hours. Remove from the fridge 30 minutes before cooking to bring to room temperature.
2 Lightly brush barbecue grill with a little vegetable oil and preheat to high. Cook the cutlets for 5 minutes each side for medium or until cooked to your liking.
3 Meanwhile, put the reserved marinade in a small saucepan and bring to a simmer over medium heat.
4 Serve the cutlets with the mustard sauce and potato salad.

TIPS: For the mustard, use whatever you prefer or have in the fridge. A herb mustard works well. Just remember if using English mustard that it's much hotter than your average mustard.

You can marinate the cutlets for longer if you like.

Chipolatas with quesadillas

Preparation time: 15 minutes
Cooking time: 40 minutes
Serves: 4

> 2 tablespoons olive oil
> 2 garlic cloves, crushed
> 2 x 400 g (14 oz) tins diced tomatoes
> ½ teaspoon ground cumin
> 16 x 15 cm (6 in) flour tortillas
> 300 g (10½ oz/3 cups, loosely packed) coarsely
>   grated cheddar cheese
> 60 g (2¼ oz) drained bottled jalapeño chillies,
>   roughly chopped
> 20 spicy chipolatas
> coriander (cilantro) sprigs, to garnish

1 Heat the olive oil in a frying pan over medium heat and cook the garlic for 1–2 minutes or until just golden. Add the tomatoes and cumin and season well with salt and freshly ground black pepper. Reduce the heat to low and cook the relish for 30–35 minutes or until it becomes thick and pulpy.
2 Meanwhile, to make the quesadillas, sprinkle a tortilla with ⅛ of the cheese, leaving a 1 cm (½ in) border. Scatter ⅛ of the jalapeño chillies over the cheese and put another tortilla on top, pressing it down. Repeat with the remaining tortillas, cheese and jalapeños until you have eight quesadillas.
3 Preheat barbecue flat plate and grill to low. Cook the chipolatas on the flat plate, turning occasionally, for 10–12 minutes or until cooked through. When the chipolatas are nearly ready, begin cooking the quesadillas on the grill for 1–2 minutes on each side or until the cheese melts.
4 Cut each quesadilla into quarters and serve with the tomato relish and chipolatas, garnished with the coriander.

TIP: You may need to cook the quesadillas in batches. To keep the cooked ones warm, loosely cover with foil and keep near the barbecue.

Whole barbecued sirloin with horseradish cream & salsa verde

Preparation time: 10 minutes (+ standing time)
Cooking time: 30 minutes
Serves: 6

1.6 kg (3 lb 8 oz) piece beef sirloin
1 tablespoon olive oil
salsa verde (see page 123), to serve
mashed potato (optional), to serve

Horseradish cream
245 g (8¾ oz/1 cup) sour cream
90 g (3¼ oz/⅓ cup) bought horseradish

1 Remove the sirloin from the fridge and bring to room temperature.

2 Preheat barbecue flat plate to high. Season the sirloin generously with sea salt and drizzle with the olive oil. Cook for 6 minutes, turning to brown each side.

3 Remove the sirloin from the heat and place a stainless steel rack on top of the flat plate, then place the sirloin on the rack (to raise the meat away from the direct heat).

4 Reduce the heat to medium–low and cook with the barbecue lid down for 20 minutes for medium–rare (a meat thermometer inserted in the centre of the sirloin should read 58°C/136°F) or until cooked to your liking (see tip). Transfer the sirloin to a clean plate, loosely cover with foil and set aside to rest in a warm place for 10 minutes.

5 Meanwhile, to make the horseradish cream, put the sour cream and horseradish in a bowl, mix to combine and season with a little salt.

6 Carve the sirloin into thick slices and serve with the horseradish cream, salsa verde and mashed potato, if desired.

TIP: You will need a covered barbecue for this recipe. If you have a temperature gauge or oven thermometer you can put it in the barbecue. The temperature should be about 140-150°C (275-300°F) when the lid is down.

Lamb

Barbecued lamb cutlets with oregano & pepper

Preparation time: 15 minutes (+ 30 minutes marinating time)
Cooking time: 20 minutes
Serves: 4

185 ml (6 fl oz/¾ cup) olive oil
60 ml (2 fl oz /¼ cup) freshly squeezed lemon juice
⅓ cup oregano leaves (smaller leaves left as sprigs)
1½ teaspoons coarsely cracked black pepper
8–12 lamb cutlets (about 750 g/1 lb 10 oz in total)
2 zucchini (courgettes), cut into 2.5 cm (1 in) pieces
1 large red capsicum (pepper), seeded, cut
   into 2.5 cm (1 in) pieces
1 large eggplant (aubergine), cut into
   2.5 cm (1 in) pieces
250 g (9 oz) cherry tomatoes on the vine
50 g (1¾ oz) wild rocket (arugula)

Dressing
60 ml (2 fl oz/¼ cup) extra virgin olive oil
1 tablespoon white wine vinegar
sea salt, to taste

1 Put 125 ml (4 fl oz/½ cup) of the olive oil, the lemon juice, oregano and pepper in a non-reactive dish. Add the lamb cutlets and turn to coat, then cover and marinate in the fridge for 30 minutes.
2 Meanwhile, to make the dressing, combine all the ingredients in a jar and shake well. Set aside.
3 Preheat barbecue grill and flat plate to medium–high. Toss the zucchini, capsicum and eggplant in the remaining olive oil and season well with salt. Cook on the flat plate for 15 minutes, turning occasionally, or until charred and tender. Place the cherry tomatoes on the flat plate in the last 3 minutes just to warm through.
4 Meanwhile, remove the cutlets from the marinade and season with salt. Cook on the grill for 2 minutes each side for medium or until cooked to your liking.
5 Serve the cutlets with the barbecued vegetables, warm tomatoes and rocket, and drizzled with the dressing.

Greek marinated butterflied leg of lamb

Preparation time: 5 minutes (+ overnight marinating
and 15 minutes standing time)
Cooking time: 20 minutes
Serves: 6

1 lemon
60 ml (2 fl oz/¼ cup) olive oil
5 garlic cloves, thinly sliced
1 tablespoon dried oregano
1.2 kg (2 lb 10 oz) butterflied leg of lamb (see tip)
barbecued potatoes, and lemon wedges, to serve

Dressing
2 tablespoons extra virgin olive oil
1 tablespoon freshly squeezed lemon juice
1 garlic clove, crushed
2 tablespoons roughly chopped oregano leaves

TIPS: Butterflying the
leg helps to infuse the
marinade through the
meat and cuts back on
cooking time.

You will need a covered
barbecue for this recipe.

1 Use a vegetable peeler to remove the zest from the lemon and then juice the lemon. Combine the lemon zest and juice, olive oil, garlic and oregano in a large, shallow non-reactive dish. Add the lamb and season with freshly ground black pepper. Turn to coat, then cover and marinate in the fridge overnight.

2 Meanwhile, to make the dressing, combine all the ingredients in a small bowl and season with sea salt and freshly ground black pepper.

3 Preheat covered barbecue flat plate to high (see tip). Season the lamb with salt and barbecue for 2–3 minutes each side or until browned.

4 Remove the lamb and place a stainless steel rack on top of the flat plate, then place the lamb on the rack (to raise the meat away from the direct heat). Reduce the heat to medium, lower the lid and cook for 15–20 minutes for medium, turning halfway through and brushing occasionally with the marinade, or until cooked to your liking. Transfer the lamb to a clean plate and drizzle with half the dressing. Loosely cover with foil and set aside in a warm place for 15 minutes to rest.

5 Serve the carved lamb with the remaining dressing, the potatoes and lemon wedges.

Lamb kofta

Preparation time: 15 minutes (+ 20 minutes chilling time)
Cooking time: 15 minutes
Serves: 4

500 g (1 lb 2 oz) minced (ground) lamb
1 small brown onion, finely chopped
1 egg
30 g (1 oz/¼ cup) dry breadcrumbs
2 garlic cloves, crushed
3 teaspoons ground cumin
2 teaspoons finely grated lemon zest
¼ cup finely chopped mint
olive oil, for brushing
Lebanese bread, tabouleh and plain
  yoghurt, to serve
mint sprigs (optional), to garnish

1 Combine the lamb, onion, egg, breadcrumbs, garlic, cumin, lemon zest and mint in a large bowl and season with salt and freshly ground black pepper. Divide the mixture into four then use wet hands to shape each quarter onto a long metal skewer to form a 20 cm (8 in) kofta. Cover and refrigerate for 20 minutes.
2 Lightly brush barbecue flat plate with a little olive oil and preheat to medium–high. Cook the koftas for 10–12 minutes, turning regularly, or until cooked through and lightly charred.
3 Serve the koftas on the Lebanese bread with the tabouleh and a dollop of yoghurt. Garnish with mint sprigs, if using.

Sumac-spiced lamb wraps

Preparation time: 20 minutes
Cooking time: 10 minutes
Serves: 4

olive oil, for brushing
1 tablespoon ground sumac (see tip)
½ teaspoon freshly ground black pepper
2 lamb backstraps (loin fillet), trimmed
1 avocado, peeled, stone removed, diced
2 ripe tomatoes, diced
½ red onion, diced
1 cup roughly chopped flat-leaf (Italian) parsley
2 tablespoons extra virgin olive oil
1 tablespoon freshly squeezed lemon juice
Tabasco sauce, to taste
4 thin wholemeal (whole-wheat) bread wraps

1 Lightly oil barbecue flat plate with a little olive oil and preheat to medium.

2 Put the sumac, black pepper and sea salt to taste in a plastic bag and shake to combine. Add the lamb backstraps and shake several times until the lamb is well coated in the spices.

3 Cook the lamb for 5 minutes. Turn the lamb over and cook for another 4 minutes. Transfer to a clean plate, loosely cover with foil and set aside in a warm place for 5 minutes to rest.

4 Meanwhile, put the avocado, tomato, onion and parsley in a large bowl and gently toss to combine. Combine the extra virgin olive oil, lemon juice and a few drops of Tabasco sauce in a small bowl. Pour over the avocado mixture and toss to coat. Season with sea salt, freshly ground black pepper and a little extra Tabasco, if desired.

5 Finely slice the lamb and divide it between the bread wraps. Top with the avocado mixture, roll up, cut in half and serve.

TIP: Sumac is a spice made from crushing the dried sumac berry. It has a mild lemony flavour and is widely used throughout the Middle East. It is available at selected supermarkets and delicatessens.

Lamb cutlets with ginger nori butter

Preparation time: 20 minutes (+ 3 hours marinating time)
Cooking time: 1 hour
Serves: 4

125 ml (4 fl oz/½ cup) Japanese plum wine (see tip)
2 tablespoons soy sauce
1 teaspoon finely grated fresh ginger
2 garlic cloves, crushed
¼ teaspoon sesame oil
16 lamb cutlets (about 1 kg/2 lb 4 oz in total)
4 small orange sweet potatoes
  (about 800 g/1 lb 12 oz in total)
2 teaspoons vegetable oil, plus extra, for brushing
Asian leaf salad, to serve

Ginger nori butter
90 g (3¼ oz) butter, softened
1½ tablespoons very finely shredded nori
2 teaspoons finely grated fresh ginger

> **TIPS:** Japanese plum wine is available from speciality Japanese grocery stores and some liquor suppliers. You can use plum juice.
>
> You will need a covered barbecue for this recipe. To cook on your barbecue using indirect heat, preheat one half of the barbecue with the burners at opposite ends (see tip page 8).

1 Combine the plum wine, soy sauce, ginger, garlic and sesame oil in a shallow non-reactive dish. Add the cutlets and turn to coat, then cover and marinate in the fridge for 3 hours.

2 Meanwhile, to make the ginger nori butter, use a fork to mash the butter, nori and ginger together in a small bowl. Season with freshly ground black pepper.

3 Preheat half a covered barbecue to medium (see tip). Brush the sweet potatoes with vegetable oil, wrap them in a double layer of foil then put them on the barbecue over the burners that aren't turned on and lower the lid. Roast for 50 minutes or until tender when pierced with a sharp knife, then remove from the heat and leave the barbecue uncovered. Set the sweet potatoes aside in a warm place. Preheat the barbecue grill to medium–high.

4 Drain the marinade into a small saucepan and boil it over high heat for 5 minutes or until it is reduced by about half. Brush barbecue grill with a little extra vegetable oil and cook the cutlets on the grill for 2 minutes, then turn them over, brush with the reduced marinade and cook for another 1–2 minutes for medium or until cooked to your liking.

5 Remove the cutlets from the barbecue, transfer to a clean plate and brush with the remaining reduced marinade. Loosely cover with foil and set aside in a warm place for 3 minutes to rest.

6 Serve the lamb and Asian leaf salad with the sweet potatoes topped with the nori butter.

Lemony lamb loin chops with chargrilled zucchini & asparagus

Preparation time: 20 minutes (+ 1 hour marinating time)
Cooking time: 10 minutes
Serves: 4

80 ml (2½ fl oz/⅓ cup) freshly squeezed
   lemon juice
2 tablespoons olive oil
1 teaspoon lemon thyme leaves
1 garlic clove, crushed
8 lamb loin chops (about 1 kg/2 lb 4 oz in total)
130 g (4½ oz/½ cup) Greek-style yoghurt
2 tablespoons finely chopped mint
3 zucchini (courgettes), trimmed, thickly
   sliced diagonally
350 g (12 oz/2 bunches) asparagus, trimmed,
   thickly sliced diagonally

1 Combine half the lemon juice, 1½ tablespoons of the olive oil, the thyme leaves and garlic in a large non-reactive dish. Add the lamb and turn to coat, then cover and marinate in the fridge for at least 1 hour.

2 Combine the yoghurt and mint in a small bowl and season with salt and freshly ground black pepper.

3 Combine the zucchini and asparagus in a large bowl with the remaining olive oil and toss to coat.

4 Preheat barbecue flat plate and grill to medium. Cook the asparagus and zucchini on the flat plate for 6–8 minutes, turning occasionally, or until lightly charred and just tender. Remove from the barbecue and place in a large bowl with the remaining lemon juice.

5 Meanwhile, season the lamb with salt and cook on the grill for 8 minutes for medium, turning halfway through, or until cooked to your liking. Transfer the lamb to a clean plate, loosely cover with foil and set aside in a warm place for 3 minutes to rest.

6 Serve the lamb with the barbecued vegetables and a dollop of the minted yoghurt.

Lamb cutlets with spicy sesame sprinkle

Preparation time: 20 minutes
Cooking time: 15 minutes
Serves: 4

2 tablespoons sesame seeds
½ teaspoon cumin seeds
½ teaspoon dried oregano
½ teaspoon dried red chilli flakes
½ teaspoon sea salt flakes
2 red capsicums (peppers), seeded,
　cut into eighths
2 red onions, cut into eighths
2 tablespoons extra virgin olive oil
½ cup basil leaves
2 tablespoons caramelised balsamic
　vinegar (see tip)
12–16 lamb cutlets
green salad, to serve

TIP: Caramelised balsamic vinegar (also called balsamic glaze and reduced balsamic) is a thick, sweetened aged balsamic vinegar and is available at selected delicatessens and speciality food stores. You can replace it in this recipe with 4 tablespoons balsamic vinegar simmered with 1 tablespoon sugar until reduced by half.

1 Place the sesame seeds, cumin seeds, oregano and chilli flakes in a small frying pan over medium heat and cook for 3 minutes or until the sesame seeds are golden. Remove from the heat, put in a mortar and use the pestle to grind to a coarse powder. Add the sea salt and grind the salt into the spices. Spoon into a small serving bowl.

2 Preheat barbecue flat plate and grill to medium.

3 Put the capsicum, onion and half the olive oil in a large bowl and toss to coat. Cook the vegetables on the flat plate for 6 minutes, tossing occasionally, or until lightly charred and tender. Transfer the vegetables to a bowl with the basil leaves and balsamic vinegar and toss to coat.

4 Meanwhile, brush the cutlets with the remaining oil and season with salt. Cook on the grill for 2 minutes each side for medium or until cooked to your liking. Transfer to a clean plate, loosely cover with foil and set aside in a warm place to rest for a few minutes.

5 Serve the cutlets with the capsicum salad, green salad and a generous sprinkle of the spicy sesame sprinkle.

Rosemary & lemon lamb sausages

Preparation time: 15 minutes (+ 20 minutes chilling time)
Cooking time: 10 minutes
Serves: 4

700 g (1 lb 9 oz) minced (ground) lamb
1 small brown onion, finely chopped
1 garlic clove, crushed
2 teaspoons finely chopped rosemary leaves,
   plus extra sprigs, to garnish
2 teaspoons finely grated lemon zest
1 teaspoon smoked paprika
20 g (¾ oz/⅓ cup, lightly packed) fresh breadcrumbs
1 egg
8 thin prosciutto slices, halved widthways
olive oil, for brushing
mashed potato and green salad, to serve

1 Combine the lamb, onion, garlic, rosemary, lemon zest, paprika, breadcrumbs and egg in a large bowl and season with salt and freshly ground black pepper. Mix until well combined then divide mixture into eight equal portions. Roll each portion into a 15 cm (6 in) long sausage.

2 Place two half slices of prosciutto slightly overlapping on a clean chopping board. Top with a sausage and roll tightly to enclose. Repeat with the remaining prosciutto and sausages. Refrigerate for 20 minutes.

3 Lightly oil barbecue grill with a little olive oil and preheat to medium–high. Cook the sausages for 10 minutes, turning regularly, or until browned and cooked through. Serve with the mashed potato and salad. Garnish with rosemary sprigs.

TIP: The uncooked sausages will keep in an airtight container in the freezer for up to 2 months.

Hoisin lamb with Asian rice salad

Preparation time: 30 minutes (+ 4 hours marinating time)
Cooking time: 30 minutes
Serves: 4

60 ml (2 fl oz/¼ cup) hoisin sauce
2 tablespoons soy sauce
2 garlic cloves, bruised
1 tablespoon finely grated fresh ginger
2 teaspoons peanut oil
800 g (1 lb 12 oz) lamb backstraps
 (loin fillet), trimmed
16 spring onions (scallions),
 trimmed to 18 cm (7 in) long
40 g (1½ oz/¼ cup) coarsely chopped
 roasted unsalted peanuts

2 tablespoons peanut oil
1 large red onion, finely chopped
4 garlic cloves, crushed
1 tablespoon finely chopped fresh ginger
1 fresh long red chilli, seeded, thinly sliced
4 spring onions (scallions), thinly sliced
2 tablespoons soy sauce
1 tablespoon freshly squeezed lime juice
2 teaspoons balsamic vinegar
½ teaspoon sesame oil
1 cup coriander (cilantro) leaves

Asian rice salad
1.25 litres (44 fl oz/5 cups) water
400 g (14 oz/2 cups) long-grain white rice

1 Combine the hoisin sauce, soy sauce, garlic, ginger and 1 teaspoon of the peanut oil in a shallow non-reactive dish. Add the lamb and turn to coat, then cover and marinate in the fridge for 4 hours or overnight.

2 To make the Asian rice salad, bring the water to the boil in a large saucepan. Add the rice and cook, uncovered, for 12–15 minutes over low heat or until tender. Drain and rinse the rice under cold running water then transfer to a large bowl. While the rice is cooking, heat the peanut oil in a frying pan over medium heat. Add the onion, garlic, ginger and chilli and cook for 5–6 minutes or until the onion is soft but not brown. Stir in the spring onion and cook for another minute. Remove from the heat and add the onion mixture to the rice with the soy sauce, lime juice, balsamic vinegar, sesame oil and coriander and mix well. Cover the salad and refrigerate until ready to serve.

3 Toss the spring onion with the remaining oil and season well. Remove the lamb from the marinade and season. Pour the marinade into a small saucepan and simmer for 5 minutes or until slightly reduced. Preheat barbecue flat plate to medium heat. Cook the lamb for 6–7 minutes each side for medium or until cooked to your liking, brushing it frequently with the reduced marinade. Transfer to a clean plate, loosely cover with foil and set aside to rest in a warm place for 3 minutes. Meanwhile, cook the spring onion on the flat plate for 1–2 minutes or until tender but still firm.

4 Cut the lamb across the grain into thick slices and arrange on a plate. Drizzle any juices over the lamb and sprinkle with the peanuts. Serve with the spring onions and rice salad.

Pork

Mexican pork chops with corn salsa

Preparation time: 20 minutes
Cooking time: 10 minutes
Serves: 4

2 tablespoons olive oil
35 g (1¼ oz) packet taco seasoning
finely grated zest and freshly squeezed
   juice of 1 lime
4 pork chops (about 225 g/8 oz each)
lime wedges, to serve

Corn salsa
3 corn cobs, in husks
olive oil spray
2 small vine-ripened tomatoes, roughly diced
1 small red onion, finely chopped
1 Lebanese (short) cucumber, roughly diced
⅓ cup chopped coriander (cilantro)
2 tablespoons freshly squeezed lime juice
1 tablespoon olive oil

> **TIP:** Microwaving the corn in the husks helps to create steam, cooking the corn faster.

1 Microwave the corn cobs, in husks, on high for 3 minutes (see tip). Set aside for 5 minutes or until cool enough to handle then remove the husks and silks.

2 Meanwhile, combine the olive oil, taco seasoning, lime zest and juice in a large bowl. Add the pork chops and toss to coat in the spice mixture.

3 Preheat barbecue grill to medium–high. Cook the chops for 3–4 minutes each side until just cooked through. Transfer the chops to a clean plate, loosely cover with foil and set aside in a warm place for a few minutes to rest.

4 Meanwhile, to make the corn salsa, spray the corn with oil spray. Cook the corn alongside the pork for 4–5 minutes, turning, or until golden. Cut the cobs in half and then use a sharp knife to remove the kernels. Combine the kernels in a medium bowl with the remaining ingredients.

5 Serve the pork chops topped with the corn salsa and lime wedges.

Chorizo & haloumi skewers

Preparation time: 40 minutes (+ 30 minutes soaking time)
Cooking time: 8 minutes
Makes: 12

2 chorizo sausages (about 150 g/5½ oz each) (see tip)
2 x 180 g (6¼ oz) packets haloumi cheese
1 lemon
olive oil, for brushing

Lemon & mint dressing
2 tablespoons extra virgin olive oil
½ teaspoon finely grated lemon zest
1 tablespoon freshly squeezed lemon juice
1½ tablespoons chopped mint

1 Soak 12 wooden skewers in cold water for 30 minutes to prevent scorching.

2 Cut the chorizo and haloumi into 24 bite-sized pieces each. Cut the lemon into 12 wedges, then slice each wedge in half crossways. Thread the chorizo, haloumi and lemon pieces alternately onto the soaked wooden skewers.

3 To make the lemon & mint dressing, whisk together all the ingredients in a small bowl. Season with salt and freshly ground black pepper to taste and set aside.

4 Lightly brush barbecue flat plate with a little olive oil and preheat to medium. Cook the skewers for 8 minutes, turning occasionally or until the chorizo and haloumi are heated through and the skewers are lightly charred. Spoon the dressing over the hot skewers and serve immediately.

TIP: Chorizo sausages are made from highly seasoned minced (ground) pork and are flavoured with garlic, chilli and a number of other spices. They are available from selected supermarkets, delicatessens and butchers.

Adobo pork with coconut rice

Preparation time: 25 minutes (+ 3 hours marinating time)
Cooking time: 20 minutes
Serves: 6

170 ml (5½ fl oz/⅔ cup) balsamic vinegar
80 ml (2½ fl oz/⅓ cup) soy sauce
3 fresh bay leaves
4 garlic cloves, crushed
½ teaspoon freshly ground black pepper
6 pork cutlets
2 tablespoons peanut oil
grilled mango cheeks (see tip), lime cheeks
  and salad leaves, to serve

Coconut rice
400 g (14 oz/2 cups) jasmine rice
2 tablespoons peanut oil
1 small brown onion, finely diced
1 teaspoon finely grated fresh ginger
2 garlic cloves, crushed
625 ml (21½ fl oz/2½ cups) coconut milk

TIP: To prepare the grilled mango cheeks, brush the mango cheeks with a little peanut oil and cook on the preheated high barbecue grill or flat plate for 1-2 minutes or until charred and warmed.

1 Combine the balsamic vinegar, soy sauce, bay leaves, garlic and black pepper in a shallow non-reactive dish. Add the pork and turn to coat then cover and refrigerate for at least 3 hours or overnight.

2 To make the coconut rice, rinse the rice under cold running water until the water runs clear. Heat the peanut oil in a medium heavy-based saucepan over medium heat, then add the onion, ginger and garlic. Cook for 3 minutes or until the onion is soft, then add the rice and stir for 1 minute or until the rice is coated in oil. Stir in the coconut milk, bring to the boil, then turn the heat down as low as possible and cook very gently, covered, for 15 minutes. Remove the pan from the heat and set aside, covered, for 5 minutes. Use a fork to gently stir and separate the grains. Season well with salt and freshly ground black pepper.

3 Meanwhile, preheat barbecue grill to medium. Remove the pork from the marinade and pat dry with paper towel. Brush both sides of the pork with the peanut oil and season lightly with salt and freshly ground black pepper. Cook the pork for 8 minutes each side or until just cooked through. Transfer to a clean plate, loosely cover with foil and set aside in a warm place for 4 minutes to rest. Serve with the coconut rice, grilled mango, lime cheeks and salad leaves.

Vietnamese pork kebabs with chilli lime pickle

Preparation time: 40 minutes (+ 30 minutes soaking
and 2 hours marinating time)
Cooking time: 15 minutes
Serves: 4

2 pork fillets (about 400 g/14 oz each), trimmed,
   cut into 36 chunks in total
6 spring onions (scallions)
2 garlic cloves, crushed
1 tablespoon caster (superfine) sugar
2 tablespoons fish sauce
¼ teaspoon freshly ground white pepper
1 tablespoon peanut oil
350 g (12 oz) dried flat rice noodles
1 baby cos (romaine) lettuce, leaves separated
2 tablespoons coriander (cilantro) leaves

Chilli lime pickle
125 g (4½ oz/½ cup) hot lime pickle
130 g (4½ oz/½ cup) thick plain yoghurt
1 bird's eye chilli, seeded, finely chopped
1 tablespoon chopped coriander (cilantro) leaves

1 Soak 12 wooden skewers in cold water for 30 minutes to prevent scorching.

2 Thread three pieces of pork onto each skewer and place in a shallow non-reactive dish. Finely chop four of the spring onions, put in a mortar with the garlic and caster sugar and use the pestle to grind to a coarse paste. Mix in the fish sauce, white pepper and peanut oil. Pour over the pork kebabs, turning to coat. Cover and refrigerate for 2 hours.

3 Meanwhile, put all the chilli lime pickle ingredients in a food processor and blend until smooth. Refrigerate, covered, until ready to serve.

4 Cook the noodles in a large saucepan of boiling water for 4–5 minutes or until tender. Drain and place in a covered bowl at room temperature until needed.

5 Preheat barbecue grill to high. Cook the kebabs for 3–4 minutes each side or until the pork is just cooked through.

6 Cut the remaining spring onions lengthways into fine strips. Line serving plates with the lettuce leaves and put a nest of noodles on top. Put three pork skewers on each plate and scatter with the spring onion strips and coriander leaves. Serve with a dollop of the chilli lime pickle on the side.

Asian sticky pork ribs

Preparation time: 15 minutes (+ 3 hours marinating
and 30 minutes standing time)
Cooking time: 20 minutes
Serves: 4 as a main or 8 as finger food

> 60 g (2¼ oz/⅓ cup, lightly packed) brown sugar
> 60 ml (2 fl oz/¼ cup) kecap manis (see tip)
> 60 ml (2 fl oz/¼ cup) freshly squeezed lime juice
> 1½ tablespoons finely grated fresh ginger
> 1 tablespoon vegetable oil
> 1 teaspoon Chinese five-spice
> 3 garlic cloves, crushed
> 1 kg (2 lb 4 oz) American-style pork ribs

1 Combine the brown sugar, kecap manis, lime juice, ginger,
oil, five-spice and garlic in a shallow non-reactive dish. Add
the pork ribs, toss to coat, then cover and refrigerate
for 3 hours or overnight.
2 Remove the ribs from the fridge and bring to room
temperature 30 minutes before cooking.
3 Preheat barbecue flat plate to medium. Cook the ribs for
20 minutes, turning every 5 minutes and brushing with the
marinade, or until caramelised and just cooked through.
4 Serve cut into smaller portions, if desired.

TIP: Kecap manis is a
thick, sweet Indonesian
soy sauce. It is available
from supermarkets in the
Asian section.

Roast pork loin with fig & pecan stuffing

Preparation time: 20 minutes (+ 15 minutes standing time)
Cooking time: 1 hour 10 minutes
Serves: 4

50 g (1¾ oz) butter
1 small brown onion, finely chopped
35 g (1¼ oz/⅓ cup) pecans, finely chopped
30 g (1 oz/½ cup, lightly packed)
   fresh breadcrumbs
100 g (3½ oz) dried figs, finely chopped
2 tablespoons finely chopped flat-leaf
   (Italian) parsley
1 teaspoon finely grated lemon zest
1.5 kg (3 lb 5 oz) boneless rolled pork loin
   with rind
2 teaspoons olive oil
1 tablespoon sea salt flakes
1 teaspoon freshly ground black pepper
apple sauce (optional), roasted potatoes
   and green salad, to serve

> **TIP:** You will need a covered barbecue for this recipe. The barbecue needs to be very hot to start off with or the rind will not crackle. It will take about 15-20 minutes to preheat, depending on the size of the barbecue and the number of burners. The heat will increase slightly before slowly reducing to around 180°C (350°F) for the last 30 minutes of cooking.

1 Preheat covered barbecue to high until temperature gauge reaches 220°C (425°F) (see tip).

2 Heat the butter in a medium saucepan over medium heat. Add the onion and cook, stirring, for 4–5 minutes or until soft. Add the pecans and cook for 1–2 minutes or until lightly toasted. Remove from the heat, then stir in the breadcrumbs, fig, parsley and lemon zest.

3 Unroll the pork and place on a chopping board, rind-side down. Starting from the centre, cut through the thickest part of the meat to butterfly. Press the stuffing mixture against the loin along the width of the pork. Roll the pork to enclose the stuffing and secure with kitchen string at 2 cm (¾ in) intervals.

4 Place the rolled pork on a wire rack in a large disposable foil baking dish and pour in enough water to come 2 cm (¾ in) up the side of the dish. Rub the pork with the olive oil then rub the sea salt and black pepper into the rind. Place the dish on the barbecue flat plate and lower the hood. Reduce heat to medium and cook for 1 hour, adding extra water to the dish if necessary as it evaporates. Remove the pork from the barbecue, loosely cover with foil and set aside in a warm place for 15 minutes to rest.

5 Serve the pork with the apple sauce, if using, roasted potatoes and salad.

Soy & chilli marinated pork fillet with orange & mint salad

Preparation time: 30 minutes (+ 3 hours marinating time)
Cooking time: 10 minutes
Serves: 6

60 ml (2 fl oz/¼ cup) soy sauce
60 g (2¼ oz/¼ cup, firmly packed) brown sugar
2 garlic cloves, crushed
2 fresh long red chillies, seeded, finely chopped
2 tablespoons finely grated fresh ginger
2 pork fillets (about 800 g/1 lb 12 oz in total)
  (see tip), trimmed
6 oranges, segmented, juice reserved
60 ml (2 fl oz/¼ cup) extra virgin olive oil
⅔ cup mint leaves
½ red onion, thinly sliced
1 bunch watercress, leaves picked, washed

1 Combine the soy sauce, brown sugar, garlic, chilli and ginger in a large non-reactive dish. Add the pork and turn to coat then cover and marinate in the fridge for 3 hours.
2 Preheat barbecue flat plate to medium. Cook the pork for 10 minutes, turning frequently and brushing with the marinade, or until just cooked through. Transfer to a clean plate, loosely cover with foil and set aside in a warm place to rest for a few minutes.
3 Combine the orange segments and juice, olive oil, mint leaves, onion, watercress and any meat juices. Cut the pork into thin slices, add to the salad and toss gently to combine. Serve immediately.

TIP: To avoid the thinner part of the fillet overcooking, cut it off and cook it for 7-8 minutes only.

Pork cutlets with pears & potatoes

Preparation time: 10 minutes
Cooking time: 25 minutes
Serves: 4

> 4 pork loin cutlets (about 200 g/7 oz each)
> 15 thyme sprigs, leaves picked
> 125 ml (4 fl oz/½ cup) olive oil
> 2 tablespoons balsamic vinegar
> 1 tablespoon dijon mustard
> 1 tablespoon brown sugar
> 600 g (1 lb 5 oz) small desiree potatoes (or other
>   waxy potatoes), peeled and quartered
> 2 firm, ripe pears, each cut into 8 wedges
> 1 red onion, cut into wedges
> ½ radicchio lettuce (red chicory), leaves
>   separated, washed

1 Preheat barbecue flat plate and grill to medium–high. Season the pork cutlets with sea salt and freshly ground black pepper. Combine the thyme with 1 tablespoon of the olive oil and brush over the cutlets.

2 Place 80 ml (2½ fl oz/⅓ cup) of the olive oil, the balsamic vinegar, mustard and sugar in a small bowl and whisk to combine. Toss the potato, pear and onion with the remaining olive oil and season generously. Cook on the barbecue flat plate for 15 minutes, turning occasionally, or until golden. Drizzle over half of the olive oil and balsamic dressing and cook for another 10 minutes or until tender (the potato may take a little longer than the pear and onion).

3 Meanwhile, cook the cutlets on the barbecue grill for 4 minutes each side or until just cooked through. Transfer to a clean plate, loosely cover with foil and set aside in a warm place for 3 minutes to rest.

4 Serve the cutlets with the potato, pear, onion and radicchio leaves, and drizzle with the remaining dressing.

Chicken

Chicken & prosciutto skewers

Preparation time: 15 minutes (+ 30 minutes soaking time)
Cooking time: 25 minutes
Serves: 4

175 g (6 oz/1 bunch) asparagus, trimmed
800 g (1 lb 12 oz) skinless chicken breast fillets,
   trimmed, cut into 5 cm (2 in) pieces
8 thick prosciutto or pancetta slices, cut into
   5 cm (2 in) wide lengths
16 thyme sprigs
olive oil, for brushing
2 zucchini (courgettes), thinly sliced lengthways
½ green coral lettuce, leaves separated, washed
120 g (4¼ oz) soft goat's cheese

Lemon dressing
80 ml (2½ fl oz/⅓ cup) extra virgin olive oil
1½ tablespoons freshly squeezed lemon juice
pinch of sugar

1 Soak eight wooden skewers in cold water for 30 minutes to prevent scorching.

2 Cook the asparagus in boiling salted water for 2 minutes or until bright green and tender-crisp. Refresh in iced water. Cut in half lengthways and set aside.

3 Thread the chicken and prosciutto alternately onto the skewers, roughly threading the thyme in the gaps between the chicken and the prosciutto. Brush with olive oil and season with salt.

4 Preheat barbecue grill to medium–high. Cook the zucchini for 5–6 minutes each side or until lightly charred. Set aside.

5 Cook the skewers on preheated grill for 10 minutes, turning occasionally to ensure even cooking, or until the chicken is just cooked through.

6 Meanwhile, to make the lemon dressing, combine all the ingredients in a screw-top jar and shake well.

7 Combine the asparagus, lettuce and zucchini in a salad bowl. Crumble over the goat's cheese. Season with salt and freshly ground black pepper and drizzle with the lemon dressing. Serve with the skewers.

Chicken Caesar salad

Preparation time: 30 minutes
Cooking time: 20 minutes
Serves: 4–6

4 skinless chicken thigh fillets,
  trimmed
80 ml (2½ fl oz/⅓ cup) olive oil
12 x 1 cm (½ in) thick baguette slices
1 garlic clove, halved
4 bacon slices
2 baby cos (romaine) lettuces,
  leaves separated, washed
12 drained anchovy fillets, to taste
  (optional)

Caesar dressing
1 egg yolk
1 garlic clove, crushed
3 drained anchovy fillets
1 teaspoon dijon mustard
125 ml (4 fl oz/½ cup) vegetable oil
1 tablespoon freshly squeezed
  lemon juice
½ teaspoon worcestershire sauce
2 tablespoons grated parmesan cheese

1 To make the dressing, put the egg yolk, garlic, anchovies and mustard in a food processor and blend together. With the motor running, gradually add the oil in a very thin stream and process until the mixture becomes thick. Stir in the lemon juice, worcestershire sauce and parmesan, and season to taste with salt and freshly ground black pepper.

2 Place the chicken and 1 tablespoon of the olive oil in a bowl. Season well with salt and pepper and turn to coat.

3 Preheat barbecue grill plate to medium–high. Brush the baguette slices with the remaining olive oil and toast for 1 minute each side or until crisp and lightly charred. Rub both sides of each piece of toast with the garlic and keep warm, loosely covered with foil, close to the barbecue.

4 Cook the chicken for 5 minutes each side or until just cooked through. Set aside to rest in a warm place for 2 minutes, then cut into 1 cm (½ in) strips. Cook the bacon for 3 minutes each side or until crispy, then break into 2 cm (¾ in) pieces.

5 Tear the lettuce leaves into bite-sized pieces and toss in a large bowl with the dressing, bacon, chicken and anchovies, if using. Serve with the garlic croutons.

Barbecued chicken with orange & parsley

Preparation time: 15 minutes (+ 30 minutes marinating time)
Cooking time: 10 minutes
Serves: 4

1 orange
80 ml (2½ fl oz/⅓ cup) olive oil
⅓ cup roughly chopped flat-leaf (Italian) parsley
3 garlic cloves, chopped
800 g (1 lb 12 oz) skinless chicken thigh fillets, trimmed
2 baby cos (romaine) lettuces
200 g (7 oz) small cherry tomatoes on the vine
120 g (4¼ oz) feta cheese, sliced

Dressing
80 ml (2½ fl oz/⅓ cup) extra virgin olive oil
1 tablespoon red wine vinegar
1 tablespoon freshly squeezed orange juice, strained

1 Use a sharp knife to remove the zest (without the pith) from half the orange. Finely shred the zest and place in a shallow non-reactive dish with the olive oil, parsley and garlic. Squeeze the juice from the orange and add 2 tablespoons to the marinade (reserve the remaining juice for the dressing). Add the chicken to the dish, season with sea salt and freshly ground black pepper, turn to coat, then cover and marinate in the fridge for 30 minutes.

2 Combine all the dressing ingredients in a screw-top jar and shake well. Remove the outer leaves from the lettuce, cut in half and wash thoroughly under cold running water. Remove the tomatoes from the vine, leaving the stem nearest the tomato intact. Cut most of the tomatoes in half (leave the very smallest whole).

3 Preheat barbecue grill to medium–high. Cook the chicken for 4–5 minutes each side or until just cooked through. Cut the larger thighs in half then transfer to a clean plate, loosely cover with foil and set aside in a warm place for 3 minutes to rest. Combine the lettuce, tomatoes and feta in a salad bowl. Drizzle with the dressing and serve with the chicken.

Chilli chicken with tomato & cucumber salsa

Preparation time: 10 minutes (+ 3 hours marinating time)
Cooking time: 10 minutes
Serves: 4

125 ml (4 fl oz/½ cup) freshly squeezed
    lemon juice
90 g (3¼ oz/¼ cup) honey
60 ml (2 fl oz/¼ cup) soy sauce
2 tablespoons vegetable oil
2 teaspoons sesame oil
¼ teaspoon bottled crushed chilli
1 garlic clove, crushed
2 spring onions (scallions), chopped
¼ cup finely chopped coriander (cilantro)
8 skinless chicken thigh fillets, trimmed

Tomato & cucumber salsa
1 Lebanese (short) cucumber, chopped
½ small red onion, finely chopped
1 ripe tomato, chopped
2 tablespoons olive oil
1 tablespoon white wine vinegar
¼ teaspoon sugar
¼ cup chopped coriander (cilantro)

1 Combine the lemon juice, honey, soy sauce, oils, chilli, garlic, spring onion, coriander and salt to taste in a large non-reactive dish. Add the chicken and turn to coat, then cover and marinate in the fridge for at least 3 hours or overnight.
2 Preheat barbecue grill to high. Drain the chicken, reserving the marinade. Cook the chicken, brushing occasionally with the reserved marinade, for 5 minutes each side or until tender and just cooked through.
3 Meanwhile, to make the tomato salsa, combine all the ingredients in a large bowl and season with salt and freshly ground black peper to taste, then toss gently to coat.
4 Slice the chicken and serve with the salsa.

Chicken tikka with garlic naan

Preparation time: 40 minutes (+ 4 hours marinating time)
Cooking time: 15 minutes
Serves: 4

100 g (4 oz/⅓ cup) bought tikka paste
70 g (2½ oz/¼ cup) Greek-style yoghurt
600 g (1 lb 5 oz) skinless chicken breast fillets,
   trimmed, cut into 3 cm (1¼ in) cubes
2 small red onions, quartered
vegetable oil, for brushing
2 tablespoons chopped coriander (cilantro) leaves

Apple raita
1 green apple, coarsely grated
65 g (2¼ oz/¼ cup) sour cream
¼ cup chopped mint leaves
2 teaspoons freshly squeezed lemon juice

Garlic naan
1 garlic clove, crushed
40 g (1½ oz) butter, softened
4 plain naan bread

1 Combine the tikka paste and yoghurt in a large non-reactive dish. Add the chicken and toss to coat, then cover and marinate in the fridge for 4 hours or overnight.
2 Meanwhile, soak four wooden skewers in cold water for 30 minutes to prevent scorching.
3 To make the raita, combine all the ingredients in a small bowl. Cover and refrigerate. To make the garlic naan, use a fork to mash the garlic and butter together and spread one side of each piece of naan with about 2 teaspoons of the garlic butter.
4 Preheat barbecue flat plate and grill to low–medium. Thread the chicken and onion pieces onto the skewers and cook for 5–6 minutes each side, turning once, or until just cooked through. Just before the chicken is ready, lightly brush the grill with a little oil. Cook the naan, buttered side down, for 1–2 minutes or until the bread is golden and lightly charred. Turn over and grill for 1 minute on the other side.
5 Sprinkle the skewers with the chopped coriander and serve with the garlic naan and apple raita.

Lebanese chicken

Preparation time: 30 minutes (+ overnight marinating time)
Cooking time: 20 minutes
Serves: 6

260 g (9¼ oz/1 cup) Greek-style
 yoghurt
60 ml (2 fl oz/¼ cup) freshly squeezed
 lemon juice
¼ cup roughly chopped flat-leaf (Italian)
 parsley
4 garlic cloves, crushed
3 teaspoons ground cumin
2 teaspoons brown sugar
1½ teaspoons ground coriander
1 kg (2 lb 4 oz) skinless chicken thigh fillets,
 trimmed, cut into long strips
olive oil, for brushing

Eggplant, tomato & sumac salad
2 eggplants (aubergines), cut into
 1 cm (½ in) thick rounds
100 ml (3½ fl oz) olive oil
5 large ripe tomatoes, cut into wedges
1 small red onion, thinly sliced
¼ cup roughly chopped mint
¼ cup roughly chopped flat-leaf
 (Italian) parsley
2 teaspoons sumac (see tip page 33)
2 tablespoons freshly squeezed
 lemon juice

1 Combine the yoghurt, lemon juice, parsley, garlic, cumin, sugar and coriander in a large non-reactive dish. Add the chicken strips, turn to coat, then cover and marinate in the fridge overnight.
2 Nearer to serving time, start preparing the eggplant, tomato & sumac salad. Sprinkle the eggplant with salt, place in a colander and leave for 1 hour. Rinse, drain well, then pat dry with paper towel.
3 Meanwhile, soak 12 wooden skewers in water for 30 minutes to prevent scorching.
4 Preheat the barbecue flat plate to medium. Use 2 tablespoons of the olive oil to brush the eggplant slices on both sides, then grill for 5 minutes on each side or until cooked through. Remove from the heat, allow to cool slightly and cut in half.
5 Season the chicken with salt and freshly ground black pepper then thread onto skewers. Generously brush the flat plate with olive oil and cook the chicken, turning frequently, for 8 minutes or until just cooked through.
6 Combine the eggplant, tomato, onion, mint and parsley in a bowl. Sprinkle with the sumac. Put the lemon juice and remaining olive oil in a small screw-top jar, season and shake well. Drizzle the dressing over the salad and serve with the chicken.

Chicken with corn relish

Preparation time: 20 minutes (+ cooling time)
Cooking time: 30 minutes
Serves: 4

8 boneless chicken thighs, skin on, trimmed
1 tablespoon olive oil, plus extra, for brushing
1 garlic clove, crushed
¼ teaspoon ground turmeric
½ teaspoon salt

Corn relish
200 g (7 oz/1 cup) fresh or drained tinned corn kernels
2 tablespoons olive oil
1 fresh long red chilli, seeded, finely chopped
1 small green capsicum (pepper), finely chopped
1 red onion, finely chopped
80 ml (2½ fl oz/⅓ cup) white vinegar
55 g (2 oz/¼ cup) (superfine) sugar
1 teaspoon wholegrain mustard
3 teaspoons cornflour (cornstarch)
125 ml (4 fl oz/½ cup) water
1 teaspoon sweet paprika
1 teaspoon finely chopped coriander (cilantro) leaves

TIP: Keep the corn relish for up to 4 days in an airtight container in the fridge.

1 Prick the chicken skin and put in a large frying pan of boiling water. Simmer for 5 minutes, drain and set aside to cool. Combine the olive oil, garlic, turmeric and salt and rub over the skin of the chicken.

2 To make the relish if using fresh corn, cook in boiling water for 2–3 minutes or until tender, then drain. (If using tinned corn, do not cook.) Heat 1 tablespoon of the olive oil in a saucepan over medium heat. Add the chilli, capsicum and onion and cook, stirring, for 5 minutes or until tender. Add the corn, vinegar, sugar and mustard and cook, stirring, for another 5 minutes. Blend the cornflour with the water until smooth and add to the relish. Bring to the boil, reduce the heat and stir until thickened. Stir in the paprika, coriander and remaining olive oil. Set aside to cool.

3 Lightly brush barbecue grill with a little extra olive oil and preheat to high. Cook the chicken, skin side up, for 2 minutes, then turn over and cook for 4 minutes. Cook for another 5 minutes, turning frequently, or until the chicken is well browned and just cooked through. Serve with the corn relish.

Spatchcocked marinated barbecued chicken with potato salad

Preparation time: 20 minutes (+ 8 hours or overnight marinating time)
Cooking time: 1 hour 5 minutes
Serves: 4

1.8 kg (4 lb) whole chicken, spatchcocked
80 ml (2½ fl oz/⅓ cup) olive oil
2 tablespoons balsamic vinegar
freshly squeezed juice of 1 lime
2 tablespoons chopped flat-leaf
  (Italian) parsley
2 limes, halved
sea salt, to taste
1–2 tablespoons olive oil
2 brown onions, sliced

Potato salad
600 g (1 lb 5 oz) new potatoes, halved
2 tablespoons extra virgin olive oil
1 tablespoons white wine vinegar
pinch of sugar

TIP: You will need a covered barbecue for this recipe.

1 Score the chicken through the thickest parts of the thigh and breast with a sharp knife and place the chicken in a shallow non-reactive dish. Combine the olive oil, vinegar and lime juice in a small jug. Pour half over the chicken and massage into the chicken. Place the chicken skin side down in the dish, cover and refrigerate for 8 hours or overnight. Add the parsley to the remaining oil mixture, cover and set aside.

2 Preheat a covered barbecue grill and flat plate to medium. Cook the limes, cut side down, on the flat plate for 3–4 minutes or until lightly charred, then set aside. Drain the chicken, reserving the marinade. Season the chicken with sea salt. Cook the chicken, skin side down for 5 minutes or until the skin is golden and crisp. Turn and cook, with the barbecue lid down, brushing occasionally with the reserved marinade, for 30–35 minutes or until just cooked through. Transfer to a clean plate, loosely cover with foil and set aside near the barbecue to keep warm for 10 minutes to rest.

3 Pour the oil onto the flat plate, add the onions and turn to coat in the oil. Cook for 20 minutes, stirring occasionally, to evenly caramelise the onions.

4 Meanwhile, to make the potato salad, place the potatoes in a saucepan, cover with cold water, bring to a simmer on the flat plate and cook gently for 15 minutes or until tender. Drain the potatoes, add the extra virgin olive oil and vinegar. Season with sea salt, freshly ground black pepper and the sugar and toss to coat.

5 Carve the chicken into pieces and drizzle with the oil and parsley mixture. Serve with the potato salad and grilled lime halves.

Tandoori chicken wings

Preparation time: 20 minutes (+ 3 hours marinating time)
Cooking time: 25 minutes
Serves: 4

16 small chicken wings (about 1.3 kg/3 lb in total)
90 g (3¼ oz/⅓ cup) bought tandoori paste
130 g (4½ oz/½ cup) plain yoghurt
2 tablespoons freshly squeezed lemon juice
vegetable oil, for brushing

Mint raita
190 g (6¾ oz/⅔ cup) plain yoghurt
2 tablespoons finely shredded mint
1 tablespoon freshly squeezed lemon juice

1 Cut the chicken wings into three pieces at the joints and discard the tips. Combine the tandoori paste, yoghurt and lemon juice in a large non-reactive dish. Add the chicken and toss to coat, then cover and marinate in the fridge for 3 hours.
2 To make the mint raita, place all the ingredients in a small bowl and mix until well combined. Refrigerate until required.
3 Brush the barbecue grill with the oil and preheat to low–medium. Cook the chicken wings, turning occasionally, for 20–25 minutes or until cooked through and charred (see tip). Serve the chicken wings with the raita.

TIP: Make sure the barbecue grill plate is well oiled to prevent the chicken wings from sticking. Reduce the heat to low if the wings start to brown too much.

Seafood

Lebanese snapper with tahini sauce

Preparation time: 15 minutes
Cooking time: 25 minutes
Serves: 4

1.2 kg (2 lb 10 oz) whole snapper, gutted, scaled
½ lemon, sliced
2 tablespoons olive oil
Lebanese bread and olives, to serve

Tahini sauce
200 g (7 oz/¾ cup) Greek-style yoghurt
65 g (2½ oz/¼ cup) tahini
2 tablespoons freshly squeezed lemon juice
1 tablespoon olive oil, plus extra, to serve
1 tablespoon water
chopped flat-leaf (Italian) parsley, to serve

1 Preheat barbecue grill to medium–high.

2 Season the snapper inside and out with salt and freshly ground black pepper. Place the lemon slices inside the snapper. Rub the snapper with the olive oil and place in a fish grill (see tip).

3 Cook the snapper for 25 minutes, standing the fish grill on its metal feet (to raise the flesh away from the direct heat) and turning halfway through the cooking time, or until the fish is just cooked through.

4 Meanwhile, to make the tahini sauce, combine all the ingredients in a small bowl and season with salt and freshly ground black pepper.

5 Serve the snapper with the tahini sauce drizzled with extra olive oil and sprinkled with parsley, and Lebanese bread and olives.

TIPS: If you don't have a fish grill, wrap the prepared snapper in a double layer of foil which has been sprayed with oil spray. Preheat barbecue flat plate to high. Cook the wrapped snapper for 20 minutes, turning halfway through.

The tahini sauce thickens slightly if made in advance. Stir in an extra tablespoon of water if you prefer a thinner consistency.

Swordfish steaks with mixed bean salad

Preparation time: 20 minutes (+ 1 hour marinating time)
Cooking time: 10 minutes
Serves: 4

2 tablespoons freshly squeezed lemon juice
2 tablespoons olive oil
½ teaspoon dried oregano
10 large basil leaves, roughly torn
4 swordfish steaks (about 200 g/7 oz each)
200 g (7 oz) green beans, topped
400 g (14 oz) tin cannellini beans, rinsed, drained
4 marinated artichoke hearts, cut into thin wedges
¼ cup roughly chopped flat-leaf (Italian) parsley
2 tablespoons extra virgin olive oil
lemon wedges, to serve

1 Combine the lemon juice, olive oil, oregano and basil in a large non-reactive dish.
Add the swordfish and turn to coat, then cover and marinate in the fridge for 1 hour.
2 Cook the green beans in a saucepan of boiling water for 2–3 minutes or until just tender
and bright green. Drain and rinse under cold running water.
3 Put the green beans in a large bowl with the cannellini beans, artichoke, parsley and extra
virgin olive oil. Toss to combine and season with sea salt and freshly ground black pepper.
4 Preheat barbecue flat plate to medium. Cook the swordfish for 2 minutes on each side
or until cooked to your liking.
5 Serve the swordfish with the mixed bean salad and lemon wedges.

Sesame tuna salad

Preparation time: 10 minutes (+ 2 hours 15 minutes chilling time)
Cooking time: 5 minutes
Serves: 6 as a starter

80 ml (2½ fl oz/⅓ cup) light soy sauce, plus
  2 tablespoons, extra
2 teaspoons sesame oil
1 tablespoon finely grated fresh ginger
500 g (1 lb 2 oz) piece sashimi-grade tuna
  (about 15 cm/6 in long x 8 cm/3¼ in wide)
1 tablespoon peanut oil
1½ tablespoons mirin
1 spring onion (scallion), thinly sliced, white
  and green parts separated
2 Lebanese (short) cucumbers, cut in half, seeds
  removed, thinly sliced diagonally
½ bunch watercress, leaves picked
1 tablespoon sesame seeds, toasted

1 Combine the light soy sauce, sesame oil and ginger in a shallow dish. Add the tuna and turn to coat. Cover and refrigerate for 15 minutes, turning every 5 minutes to evenly marinate.

2 Preheat barbecue flat plate to high. Remove the tuna from the marinade, place on a plate and brush with the peanut oil. Cook for 1 minute each side. Remove from the barbecue and set aside to cool to room temperature. Wrap tightly in plastic wrap and refrigerate for 2 hours or until chilled.

3 To make the dressing, combine the extra light soy sauce, mirin and the white part of the spring onion in a small bowl.

4 Arrange the cucumber on serving plates. Use a very sharp knife to thinly slice the tuna and arrange on top of the cucumber. Top with the watercress, drizzle over the dressing and sprinkle with the remaining spring onion and the sesame seeds.

Prosciutto-wrapped prawns

Preparation time: 20 minutes (+ 30 minutes
  marinating and soaking time)
Cooking time: 5 minutes
Makes: 16 as finger food

16 raw king prawns (shrimp), peeled,
  deveined, tails left intact
1 garlic clove, crushed
1 fresh long red chilli, seeded, finely
  chopped
8 prosciutto slices
2 tablespoons caramelised balsamic
  vinegar (see tip page 36)
lemon halves, to serve

1 Combine the prawns, garlic and chilli in a large non-reactive
dish and massage the marinade gently into the prawns.
Cover and refrigerate for 30 minutes. Meanwhile, soak
16 small wooden skewers in cold water for 30 minutes
to prevent scorching.

2 Cut the prosciutto slices in half crossways and lay flat on
a clean chopping board. Top each slice with a prawn then roll
the prosciutto to enclose the prawn. Insert a soaked skewer
into each prawn.

3 Preheat barbecue flat plate to medium. Cook the prawns for
2–3 minutes, turning occasionally, or until just cooked through
and lightly charred. Transfer to a serving plate, drizzle with the
balsamic vinegar and serve with the lemon halves.

TIP: To serve as a starter
for four, cook the prawns
without the skewers and
serve over 100 g (3½ oz)
mixed salad leaves and
200 g (7 oz) halved
cherry tomatoes.

Teriyaki baby octopus

Preparation time: 30 minutes (+ 30 minutes cooling
 and 4 hours or overnight marinating time)
Cooking time: 7 minutes
Serves: 4

125 ml (4 fl oz/½ cup) sake
125 ml (4 fl oz/½ cup) mirin
125 ml (4 fl oz/½ cup) dark soy sauce
1 tablespoon caster (superfine) sugar
2 teaspoons finely grated fresh ginger
2 garlic cloves, finely chopped
750 g (1 lb 10 oz) cleaned baby octopus, halved
  or quartered depending on size

Asian salad
2 sheets nori, cut into 3 cm x 5 mm (1¼ x ¼ in) pieces
2 tablespoons mirin
1 tablespoon freshly squeezed lemon juice
½ teaspoon sesame oil
2 teaspoons canola oil
100 g (3½ oz) mixed baby Asian greens
100 g (3½ oz) snow pea (mangetout) sprouts
2 Lebanese (short) cucumbers, thinly sliced lengthways
  with a vegetable peeler
½ daikon (500 g/1 lb 2 oz), thinly sliced with a mandolin
2 fresh long red chillies, seeded, thinly sliced lengthways

1 Combine the sake, mirin, dark soy sauce and sugar in a small saucepan. Stir over medium heat until the sugar dissolves. Bring to the boil. Add the ginger and garlic and remove the saucepan from the heat. Leave the mixture to cool for 30 minutes.
2 Put the octopus in a large non-reactive dish. Whisk the cooled marinade, making sure it is well combined, then pour it over the octopus, stirring so that the octopus is thoroughly coated. Cover and marinate in the fridge for at least 4 hours or overnight.
3 Preheat barbecue flat plate to high. Toast the nori by holding it with tongs a few centimetres above the plate for 5 minutes or until crispy. Cut into 3 cm x 5 mm (1¼ x ¼ in) strips.
4 To make the salad, whisk together the mirin, lemon juice and oils. Toss the Asian greens, snow pea sprouts, cucumber, daikon, chilli and nori with the dressing.
5 Drain the octopus and cook on preheated flat plate for 1–2 minutes or until lightly charred and just cooked. To serve, divide the salad among serving plates and top with the warm octopus.

Barbecued prawn salad

Preparation time: 20 minutes
Cooking time: 15 minutes
Serves: 4

400 g (14 oz) new potatoes
700 g (1 lb 9 oz) raw prawns (shrimp),
  peeled, deveined
2 garlic cloves, crushed
2 tablespoons olive oil
175 g (6 oz/1 bunch) asparagus, trimmed,
  cut into 4 cm (1½ in) lengths
100 g (3½ oz) baby rocket (arugula)
1 tablespoon extra virgin olive oil
1 tablespoon freshly squeezed lemon juice

1 Cook the potatoes in a medium saucepan of boiling salted water for 15 minutes or until tender. Drain and halve.

2 Meanwhile, combine the prawns, garlic and 1 tablespoon of the olive oil in a medium bowl. Season with salt and freshly ground black pepper. Combine the asparagus and the remaining oil in a bowl and toss to coat.

3 Preheat barbecue flat plate to high. Cook the asparagus for 5 minutes, tossing occasionally, or until lightly charred and just tender. Cook the prawns alongside the asparagus for 3 minutes, tossing occasionally, or until lightly charred and prawns are just cooked through.

4 Place the rocket in a large serving bowl with the potato halves, asparagus, prawns, extra virgin olive oil and lemon juice. Gently toss to coat and serve immediately.

Warm baby octopus & watercress salad

Preparation time: 30 minutes (+ 2 hours marinating time)
Cooking time: 5 minutes
Serves: 6 as a starter or light main

2 tablespoons olive oil
1 teaspoon dried oregano
3 garlic cloves, thinly sliced
finely grated zest and freshly squeezed
   juice of 1 lemon
800 g (1 lb 12 oz) baby octopus, cleaned,
   halved or quartered depending on size
½ small bunch watercress, picked
250 g (9 oz) cherry tomatoes, halved
150 g (5½ oz) baby green beans, topped
   and blanched
sliced crusty bread, to serve

TIP: Make sure the flat plate is very hot so the octopus chars rather than stews.

1 Combine the olive oil, oregano, garlic and lemon zest and juice in a large non-reactive dish. Add the octopus and toss to coat, then cover and marinate in the fridge for 2 hours.

2 Preheat barbecue flat plate to high. Season the octopus generously with salt and freshly ground black pepper. Cook for 2–3 minutes until lightly charred and tender.

3 Combine the warm octopus, watercress, tomato halves and beans in a large bowl. Season well with salt and freshly ground black pepper. Serve with the crusty bread.

Chilli ginger squid with fennel salad

Preparation time: 20 minutes (+ 1 hour marinating time)
Cooking time: 5 minutes
Serves: 4

½ teaspoon fennel seeds
1 fresh long red chilli, seeded, finely chopped
1 tablespoon finely grated fresh ginger
80 ml (2½ fl oz/⅓ cup) freshly squeezed lime juice
700 g (1 lb 9 oz) small squid tubes, cleaned
2 fennel bulbs with green fronds
2 celery stalks with leaves, thinly sliced, leaves picked
2 tablespoons extra virgin olive oil

1 Finely crush the fennel seeds using a mortar and pestle.

2 Combine the chilli, ginger, crushed fennel seeds and 2 tablespoons of the lime juice in a large non-reactive dish. Cut the squid into small strips and score with a sharp knife. Add to the chilli mixture. Toss to coat, then cover and marinate in the fridge for 1 hour.

3 Pick the fronds from the fennel and reserve. Finely slice the fennel. Put the fennel fronds and sliced fennel in a large bowl with the celery and leaves, olive oil and remaining lime juice. Toss to combine and season with sea salt and freshly ground black pepper.

4 Preheat barbecue flat plate to high. Cook the squid, turning occasionally, for 1–2 minutes or until just cooked through. Add to the fennel salad, toss to combine and serve immediately.

Barbecued salmon with gin & fennel cream

Preparation time: 25 minutes
Cooking time: 10 minutes
Serves: 6

1.2 kg (2 lb 10 oz) side of salmon, skin
  on, pin boned
2 tablespoons chopped dill
2 tablespoons chopped flat-leaf
  (Italian) parsley
½ lemon, sliced
2 tablespoons olive oil
canola oil spray
steamed potatoes and mixed leaf salad,
  to serve

Gin & fennel cream
160 g (5¾ oz/⅔ cup) sour cream
85 g (3 oz/⅓ cup) whole-egg mayonnaise
1½ tablespoons freshly squeezed lemon juice
1 tablespoon gin
1 teaspoon dijon mustard
1 teaspoon sugar
1 small fennel bulb, quartered, thinly
  sliced, green fronds reserved

1 To make the gin & fennel cream, put the sour cream, mayonnaise, lemon juice, gin, mustard and sugar in a medium bowl, season to taste with salt and freshly ground black pepper and whisk to combine. Stir in the sliced fennel and refrigerate until required.

2 Place the salmon skin side down on a clean chopping board and halve it lengthways. Season with sea salt and freshly ground black pepper. Sprinkle half of the dill and parsley over one of the sides and top with the lemon slices. Sprinkle with the remaining dill and parsley and then place the second side of salmon, skin side up, on top. Tie with kitchen string to secure and then brush generously with the olive oil. Place two large pieces of foil on top of each other on a clean chopping board and spray with the oil spray. Place the salmon in the centre and enclose in the foil.

3 Preheat barbecue flat plate to high. Cook the wrapped salmon on the flat plate for 5 minutes each side for medium, or until cooked to your liking. Carefully unwrap the foil, cut the salmon into six portions and remove the string. Serve with the gin & fennel cream garnished with the reserved fennel fronds, the potatoes and salad.

Whiting fillets wrapped in vine leaves

Preparation time: 20 minutes
Cooking time: 10 minutes
Serves: 4

> 1 lemon
> 8 whiting fillets (about 80 g/2¾ oz each)
> ½ teaspoon freshly ground white pepper
> 16–20 marinated vine leaves, drained
> 95 g (3¼ oz/½ cup) couscous
> 55 g (2 oz/⅓ cup) currants
> 2 teaspoons butter
> 125 ml (4 fl oz/½ cup) boiling water
> 1 tablespoon finely chopped preserved
>   lemon rind (see tip page 101)
> ⅓ cup chopped coriander (cilantro)
> 2 tablespoons extra virgin olive oil
> lemon halves, to serve

1 Finely grate the lemon zest and put the zest in a bowl. Use a sharp knife to remove
the remaining pith from the lemon and then cut the lemon flesh into very thin slices.
2 Place four of the whiting fillets on a clean chopping board and sprinkle with the white pepper.
Arrange the lemon flesh slices on top of the fillets then cover each with another fillet. Put four
vine leaves onto a chopping board so that they are slightly overlapping. Place one of the whiting
parcels on the leaves and then wrap the leaves around the fish. (Depending on the size of the leaves
you may need to use an extra vine leaf.) Repeat with the remaining leaves and fillets to form three
more parcels.
3 Preheat barbecue flat plate to medium.
4 Combine the couscous, currants and butter in a large bowl with the grated lemon zest and
pour over the boiling water. Cover the bowl and set aside for 3–5 minutes or until the couscous
has absorbed the water.
5 Meanwhile, cook the fish parcels for 5 minutes on each side. Transfer to a clean plate
and set aside in a warm place to rest.
6 Fluff the couscous with a fork to separate the grains, then stir through the preserved lemon and
the coriander. Divide among serving plates, top with the fish parcels and open up the vine leaves.
Drizzle with the extra virgin olive oil and serve with the lemon halves.

Vegetables & salads

Couscous & barbecued vegetable salad

Preparation time: 15 minutes
Cooking time: 15 minutes
Serves: 4 as a light meal or 6 as a side

300 g (10½ oz) pumpkin (winter squash), seeded,
  cut into 1 cm (½ in) thick wedges
2 small zucchini (courgettes), thickly sliced diagonally
1 red capsicum (pepper), thickly sliced
1 red onion, cut into wedges
1½ tablespoons Moroccan seasoning
2 tablespoons olive oil
190 g (6¾ oz/1 cup) couscous
250 ml (9 fl oz/1 cup) boiling water
½ cup roughly chopped mint
½ cup roughly chopped flat-leaf (Italian) parsley
2 tablespoons extra virgin olive oil
Greek-style yoghurt, to serve

1 Place the pumpkin, zucchini, capsicum, onion, seasoning and 1 tablespoon of the olive oil in a large bowl and toss to coat.

2 Preheat barbecue flat plate to high. Cook the vegetables, tossing occasionally, for 10–12 minutes or until lightly charred and just tender.

3 Meanwhile, combine the couscous, the remaining olive oil and the boiling water in a large bowl. Season with salt and freshly ground black pepper and stir until the water is absorbed. Cover and stand for 3 minutes or until the couscous has absorbed the water. Stir with a fork to separate the grains. Stir through the mint, parsley, extra virgin olive oil and barbecued vegetables. Serve with the yoghurt.

Barbecued haloumi & tomato salad

Preparation time: 10 minutes
Cooking time: 3 minutes
Serves: 4 as a side

150 g (5½ oz) cherry tomatoes, halved
1 tablespoon olive oil
250 g (9 oz) packet haloumi cheese,
  thickly sliced
1 tablespoon oregano leaves
60 g (2¼ oz/⅓ cup) kalamata olives
30 g (1 oz) wild rocket (arugula)

Dressing
2 tablespoons extra virgin olive oil
1 tablespoon freshly squeezed lemon juice
1 tablespoon finely chopped preserved
  lemon rind (see tip)

1 To make the dressing, combine the olive oil, lemon juice,
preserved lemon and sea salt to taste in a small bowl.
2 Sprinkle the tomato halves with sea salt to taste. Preheat
barbecue flat plate to medium–high. Drizzle the olive oil over the
flat plate and add the haloumi and tomatoes. Sprinkle with the
oregano and cook for 1 minute or until the haloumi is golden,
then turn and cook for another minute.
3 Transfer the tomatoes and haloumi to a serving plate. Top with the
olives and rocket and spoon over the dressing. Serve immediately.

TIP: Always remove
the pith and seeds from
preserved lemon before
using the rind.

Barbecued zucchini salad with mint & feta

Preparation time: 15 minutes
Cooking time: 5 minutes
Serves: 4 as a side

2 tablespoons olive oil
1 garlic clove, crushed
1 teaspoon sea salt flakes
½ teaspoon freshly ground black pepper
3 large zucchini (courgettes), cut into 1 cm
  (½ in) thick rounds
1 small red onion, thinly sliced
100 g (3½ oz) feta cheese, crumbled
½ cup mint leaves, torn
1 teaspoon finely grated lemon zest
1 tablespoon freshly squeezed lemon juice

1 Put the olive oil, garlic, sea salt and black pepper in a medium bowl and mix until well combined. Add the zucchini and toss to coat.
2 Preheat barbecue flat plate to medium–high. Cook the zucchini, turning, for 3–4 minutes or until charred and tender. Set aside for 5 minutes to cool slightly.
3 Meanwhile, combine the remaining ingredients in a large serving bowl. Add the zucchini and toss gently to combine. Serve immediately.

Jacket potatoes with avocado salsa

Preparation time: 15 minutes
Cooking time: 1 hour
Serves: 4

4 large coliban potatoes (about 1.2 kg/2 lb 10 oz in total)
olive oil spray
1 large avocado, peeled, stone removed, roughly diced
2 small vine-ripened tomatoes, roughly diced
½ small red onion, finely chopped
2 tablespoons finely chopped coriander (cilantro)
   leaves, plus extra sprigs, to garnish
1 tablespoon freshly squeezed lime juice
1 tablespoon extra virgin olive oil
2 tablespoons sour cream

1 Preheat the grill of a covered barbecue to medium.
2 Spray the unpeeled potatoes with the oil spray and wrap
in foil. Place the potatoes on the grill and cook, with the hood
down, turning occasionally, for 1 hour or until golden and
tender when pierced with a skewer.
3 Meanwhile, combine the avocado, tomato, onion,
chopped coriander, lime juice and extra virgin olive oil
in a medium bowl.
4 Remove the potatoes from the foil and cut a cross in the
tops. Squeeze each potato to open. Spoon the avocado salsa
onto the potatoes and serve topped with the sour cream and
coriander sprigs.

TIP: You will need a covered barbecue for this recipe.

Barbecued mixed vegetable salad

Preparation time: 20 minutes
Cooking time: 20 minutes
Serves: 4 as a side

　　1 red capsicum (pepper)
　　1 yellow capsicum (pepper)
　　2 zucchini (courgettes), halved
　　4 button mushrooms, quartered
　　1 brown onion, cut into wedges
　　140 g (5 oz) jap or kent pumpkin (winter squash),
　　　seeded, cut into 4 thin slices
　　2 tablespoons bought pesto
　　2 tablespoons extra virgin olive oil
　　35 g (1¼ oz) shaved parmesan cheese

1 Preheat barbecue flat plate to high. Cut the capsicums into large, flat pieces and remove the seeds and membranes. Cook skin side down for 6–8 minutes or until the skin blackens and blisters. Put in a plastic bag and leave to cool.

2 Meanwhile, cook the zucchini, mushroom, onion and pumpkin on the flat plate for 12 minutes or until cooked. Remove from the barbecue and allow to cool.

3 Peel the skin from the cooled capsicum and gently toss the flesh in a large serving bowl with the other barbecued vegetables. In a small bowl, mix together the pesto and olive oil. Season to taste with salt and freshly ground black pepper and drizzle over the vegetables. Gently toss together and serve with the parmesan scattered over.

Barbecued corn salad with jalapeño chilli, lime & coriander

Preparation time: 20 minutes
Cooking time: 20 minutes
Serves: 4 as a side dish

4 corn cobs, in husks
2 green capsicums (peppers)
80 g (2¾ oz/⅓ cup) finely chopped, drained
  bottled jalapeño chillies
80 ml (2½ fl oz/⅓ cup) extra virgin olive oil
2 tablespoons freshly squeezed lime juice
½ cup roughly chopped coriander (cilantro) leaves

1 Preheat barbecue flat plate to medium.
2 Cook the corn and whole capsicums for 20 minutes, turning occasionally, or until the corn husks and capsicums are charred on the outside. Remove from the heat. Place the capsicums in a plastic bag and leave to cool.
3 When the corn and capsicums are cool, remove the husks from the corn and cut the corn kernels from the cobs. Remove the skin and seeds from the capsicums and cut them into large dice. Put the corn kernels, capsicum, jalapeños, olive oil, lime juice and coriander into a bowl. Toss to combine and serve.

Mediterranean vegetable kebabs

Preparation time: 15 minutes
Cooking time: 15 minutes
Serves: 4 as a side

2 small zucchini (courgettes), thinly sliced
1 small eggplant (aubergine), thinly sliced,
 cut into 3 cm (1¼ in) pieces
1 large red capsicum (pepper),
 cut into 3 cm (1¼ in) pieces
1 brown onion, cut into 8 wedges
2 tablespoons olive oil

Olive & basil salsa
55 g (2 oz/⅓ cup) pitted kalamata olives
60 ml (2 fl oz/¼ cup) extra virgin olive oil
½ cup roughly chopped basil leaves

1 Combine the zucchini, eggplant, capsicum, onion and olive oil in a large bowl and season with salt and freshly ground black pepper, then toss to coat. Thread alternately onto four long metal skewers (see tip).

2 Preheat barbecue flat plate to medium–high. Cook the skewers, turning occasionally, for 15 minutes or until the vegetables are tender.

3 Meanwhile, to make the salsa, combine all the ingredients in a small bowl. Serve the skewers topped with the salsa.

TIP: Avoid threading the vegetables tightly onto the skewers as they will not cook evenly.

Barbecued asparagus with toasted pine nut dressing

Preparation time: 10 minutes
Cooking time: 15 minutes
Serves: 4 as a side dish

 40 g (1½ oz/¼ cup) pine nuts
 360 g (12¾ oz/2 bunches) asparagus, trimmed
 1 teaspoon olive oil
 1 tablespoon freshly squeezed lemon juice
 40 g (1½ oz) butter
 1 garlic clove, finely chopped

1 Toast the pine nuts in a small frying pan over low heat for 3 minutes or until golden brown. Use a mortar and pestle or a small food processor to roughly grind until just broken up.
2 Preheat barbecue flat plate to high. Combine the asparagus and olive oil in a large bowl to coat. Cook the asparagus for 6–8 minutes or until lightly charred and just tender.
3 Place the asparagus on a serving plate and drizzle with the lemon juice. Sprinkle with the crushed pine nuts.
4 Place the butter and garlic in a small frying pan and place on the barbecue. Cook for 2–3 minutes or until the butter is sizzling and turning golden brown. Pour over the asparagus and serve immediately.

Barbecued corn with chilli butter & lime

Preparation time: 10 minutes
Cooking time: 15 minutes
Serves: 6

4 corn corbs, in husks
100 g (3½ oz) butter, melted
1 teaspoon chilli flakes
10 drops Tabasco sauce, or to taste
1 lime, halved
2 tablespoons chopped coriander
  (cilantro) leaves (optional)

1 Preheat barbecue flat plate to high.
2 Strip the corn husks back and remove the silks and half of each of the husks.
3 Combine the butter, chilli flakes and Tabasco and brush half over the corn cobs. Pull the husks back up and tie with kitchen string. Cook the corn on the barbecue, turning regularly, for 12 minutes or until lightly charred and cooked. Meanwhile, cook the lime halves, flesh side down, for 3–4 minutes or until lightly coloured.
4 Transfer the corn to a serving plate, untie the husks and brush with the remaining butter mixture.
5 Sprinkle the corn with sea salt and the coriander, if using, and serve with the charred lime halves.

Marinated mushrooms with thyme

Preparation time: 10 minutes (+ 20 minutes chilling)
Cooking time: 10 minutes
Serves: 4 as a side

2 tablespoons olive oil
1 tablespoon finely chopped thyme
2 teaspoons finely grated lemon zest
1 tablespoon freshly squeezed lemon juice
2 garlic cloves, crushed
1 teaspoon sea salt flakes
½ teaspoon cracked black pepper
4 large mushroom flats, stems trimmed
lemon wedges, to serve

1 Place the olive oil, thyme, lemon zest and juice, garlic, sea salt and pepper in a small bowl and mix until well combined. Brush the oil mixture all over the mushrooms. Cover and refrigerate for 20 minutes.

2 Preheat barbecue grill to medium–high. Cook the mushrooms for 4–5 minutes each side or until charred and tender. Serve the mushrooms with the lemon wedges.

TIP: Mushroom flats are sometimes called field mushrooms. Portabello mushrooms can also be used in this recipe.

Basics

Spice rubs

Use these spice rubs to add flavour to red meat, poultry, pork or seafood before barbecuing.

Cumin & black pepper

Preparation time: 10 minutes
Cooking time: 5 minutes
Makes: ¼ cup

> 1 tablespoon cumin seeds
> 1 tablespoon coriander seeds
> 2 teaspoons fennel seeds
> 2 teaspoons black peppercorns
> 2 teaspoons sea salt flakes

Combine all the ingredients in a small heavy frying pan and place over medium–low heat. Cook for 2–3 minutes, shaking the pan occasionally, or until aromatic. Remove from the heat, then crush to a coarse powder using a mortar and pestle or small food processor. Rub on beef, chicken or pork then drizzle with olive oil before cooking.

Five-spice & chilli flakes

Preparation time: 5 minutes
Cooking time: nil
Makes: ¼ cup

> 1 tablespoon Chinese five-spice
> 1 tablespoon chilli flakes
> 1 tablespoon sea salt flakes

Combine all the ingredients in a small bowl. Sprinkle sparingly (the five-spice is quite intense) on poultry, pork or prawns (shrimp). Drizzle with peanut oil before cooking.

Lebanese seven-spice (baharat)

Preparation time: 5 minutes
Cooking time: nil
Makes: ⅓ cup

> 1 tablespoon freshly ground black pepper
> 1 tablespoon sweet paprika
> 1 tablespoon ground cumin
> 2 teaspoons ground coriander
> 2 teaspoons ground cloves
> ½ teaspoon ground cinnamon or cassia
> ¼ teaspoon ground cardamom

Combine all the ingredients in a small bowl. Rub on lamb or beef, then drizzle with olive oil before cooking.

Paprika & oregano

Preparation time: 5 minutes
Cooking time: nil
Makes: ⅓ cup

> 1 tablespoon sweet paprika
> 1 tablespoon dried oregano
> 1 tablespoon dried thyme
> 1 tablespoon brown sugar
> 1 teaspoon sea salt flakes
> ½ teaspoon cayenne pepper

Combine all the ingredients in a small bowl. Rub on beef, veal or chicken, then drizzle with olive oil before cooking.

Clockwise from top right:
Five-spice & chilli; paprika & oregano;
cumin & black pepper; and Lebanese
seven-spice (baharat).

Marinades

Chermoula

Preparation time: 10 minutes
Cooking time: nil
Makes: 185 ml (6 fl oz/¾ cup)

⅓ cup roughly chopped flat-leaf (Italian) parsley
⅓ cup roughly chopped coriander (cilantro)
zest and freshly squeezed juice of 1 lime
2 garlic cloves, crushed
1 fresh long red chilli, seeded, finely chopped
2 tablespoons olive oil
2½ teaspoons ground cumin
1 teaspoon sweet paprika
¼ teaspoon ground cinnamon

TIP: Use as a marinade for lamb, chicken or meaty fish (such as tuna or swordfish), zucchini, asparagus or mushrooms. Marinate for 30 minutes in the fridge before cooking.

Combine all the ingredients in a medium bowl.

Balsamic, caper & rosemary

Preparation time: 5 minutes
Cooking time: nil
Makes: 160 ml (5¼ fl oz/⅔ cup)

80 ml (2½ fl oz/⅓ cup) extra virgin olive oil
60 ml (2 fl oz/¼ cup) balsamic vinegar
2 tablespoons lemon juice
4 garlic cloves, crushed
3 teaspoons finely chopped rosemary leaves
2 tablespoon salted capers, rinsed, roughly chopped
2 teaspoons sea salt
½ teaspoon cracked pepper
1 teaspoon sugar

TIP: Use as a marinade for lamb, beef, zucchini or mushrooms. Marinate for 15 minutes in the fridge before cooking.

Combine all the ingredients in a medium bowl.

Vietnamese marinade

Preparation time: 10 minutes
Cooking time: nil
Makes: 185 ml (6 fl oz/¾ cup)

80 ml (2½ fl oz/⅓ cup) fish sauce
2 tablespoons oyster sauce
1 lemongrass stem, white part only, thinly sliced
zest and freshly squeezed juice of 1 lime
4 spring onions (scallions), white part only, thinly sliced
6 garlic cloves, crushed
1 teaspoon finely grated fresh ginger

TIP: Use as a marinade for chicken, pork or seafood. Marinate for 15 minutes in the fridge before cooking.

Combine all the ingredients in a medium bowl.

Sauces

Easy barbecued onion sauce

Preparation time: 5 minutes
Cooking time: 25 minutes
Makes: 1¼ cups

1 tablespoon olive oil
2 red onions, sliced into thin wedges
250 ml (9 fl oz/1 cup) tomato sauce (ketchup)
60 g (2¼ oz/¼ cup, firmly packed) brown sugar
1 tablespoon white wine vinegar
1 tablespoon worcestershire sauce
1 teaspoon sweet paprika
¼ teaspoon cayenne pepper

TIP: Serve alongside barbecued beef, veal or lamb.

Preheat barbecue flat plate to medium–high. Add the oil to the plate, top with the onions and turn with barbecue tongs to coat in the oil. Cook, stirring occasionally, for 20–25 minutes or until golden and tender. Remove from the heat, place in a bowl, add the remaining ingredients and stir to combine.

From left:
Easy barbecued onion sauce
and romesco sauce.

Sauces (continued)

Salsa verde

Preparation time: 15 minutes
Cooking time: nil
Makes: 1½ cups

> 1 small soft white bread roll
> 2 tablespoons white wine vinegar
> 2 garlic cloves, roughly chopped
> 60 g (2¼ oz/⅓ cup) salted capers, rinsed
> 8 drained anchovy fillets
> 80 g (2¾ oz/2 bunches) flat-leaf (Italian) parsley leaves, roughly chopped
> 125 ml (4 fl oz/½ cup) extra virgin olive oil

1 To make the salsa verde, break up the bread roll into small pieces and soak it in the vinegar for 2–3 minutes.
2 Put the garlic, capers, anchovies and parsley in a small food processor and process until finely chopped. Reserve 1 tablespoon of the olive oil. Add the bread and the remaining olive oil and process again until a paste forms. Season with salt and freshly ground black pepper then transfer to a serving bowl. Cover the surface with the reserved olive oil to avoid oxidisation. When ready to serve, stir to combine the extra oil.

> TIP: Serve alongside barbecued beef, veal or lamb.

Romesco sauce

Preparation time: 5 minutes
Cooking time: 20 minutes
Makes: 1¾ cups

> 2 red capsicums (peppers)
> 2 ripe roma (plum) tomatoes
> 2 fresh long red chillies
> 1 tablespoon olive oil
> 55 g (2 oz/⅓ cup) blanched almonds
> 1 tablespoon red wine vinegar
> 2 garlic cloves, chopped
> 2–3 tablespoons extra virgin olive oil

1 Preheat barbecue flat plate to high. Brush the capsicums, tomatoes and chillies with the olive oil. Cook, turning occasionally, or until the skins are blackened. The chillies will take 3–4 minutes and the tomatoes and capsicums 12–15 minutes.
2 Place the capsicums, tomatoes and chillies in a bowl, cover with plastic wrap, set aside and allow to cool slightly.
3 Peel the capsicums, tomatoes and chillies and discard the skins. Place the flesh in the bowl of a small food processor with the almonds, vinegar and garlic and process until smooth. Add the olive oil and season with sea salt and freshly ground black pepper and process again until combined.

> TIP: Serve alongside barbecued veal, lamb, pork, chicken, seafood or vegetables.

Index

Published in 2011 by Murdoch Books Pty Limited

Murdoch Books Australia
Pier 8/9
23 Hickson Road
Millers Point NSW 2000
Phone: +61 (0) 2 8220 2000
Fax: +61 (0) 2 8220 2558
www.murdochbooks.com.au

Murdoch Books UK Limited
Erico House, 6th Floor
93–99 Upper Richmond Road
Putney, London SW15 2TG
Phone: +44 (0) 20 8785 5995
Fax: +44 (0) 20 8785 5985
www.murdochbooks.co.uk

Publisher: Kylie Walker
Food Development Editor: Anneka Manning
Project Editor: Laura Wilson
Editor: Melissa Penn
Food Editor: Lucy Nunes
Design concept: Alex Frampton and Vivien Valk
Design layout: R.T.J. Klinkhamer
Photographer: Natasha Milne
Stylist: Yael Grinham
Illustrator: Alex Frampton
Production: Joan Beal

Recipe development: Michele Cranston, Sonia Greig, Cathie Lonnie and Lucy Nunes
Food preparation for photography: Julie Ballard

National Library of Australia Cataloguing-in-Publication Data
Title: Make Me Barbecue
ISBN: 978-1-74266-325-8 (pbk.)
Series: Make me.
Subjects: Barbecuing.
Dewey Number: 641.5784
A catalogue record for this book is available from the British Library.

Printed by 1010 Printing International Limited, China

CONVERSION GUIDE: We have used 20 ml (4 teaspoon) tablespoon measures. If you are
using a 15 ml (3 teaspoon) tablespoon, for most recipes the difference will not be noticeable.
However, for recipes using baking powder, gelatine, bicarbonate of soda (baking soda), small
amounts of flour and cornflour (cornstarch), add an extra teaspoon for each tablespoon specified.

On cover: Barbecued chicken with orange and parsley (page 64)